Explosive Truth Exposed

Explosive Truth Exposed

Delanie Crawford

iUniverse, Inc.
New York   Bloomington

iUniverse books may be ordered through booksellers or by contacting:

iUniverse
1663 Liberty Drive
Bloomington, IN 47403
www.iuniverse.com
1-800-Authors (1-800-288-4677)

Because of the dynamic nature of the Internet, any Web addresses or links contained in this book may have changed since publication and may no longer be valid. The views expressed in this work are solely those of the author and do not necessarily reflect the views of the publisher, and the publisher hereby disclaims any responsibility for them.

ISBN: 978-1-4401-2523-2 (sc)
ISBN: 978-1-4401-2524-9 (ebook)

Printed in the United States of America

iUniverse rev. date: 11-11-09

Contents

Author's Page

Delanie Crawford age 34 born and raised in Everett/ Seattle area, had a fun filled, sports oriented childhood, and chose Christ over drugs, gangs and alcohol. She moved to Kelso, WA at age 15, fell in love with a boy, and became rebellious against her parents and life. She dropped out of high school as a teen parent, got her G.E.D. and attended Lower Columbia College. Then she worked for four years as a mental health counselor.

Delanie began working as an exotic dancer in Portland, Oregon paying for the final touches of her education. She married a D.J. and moved to Florida, attended Saint Petersburg College and worked as an in-patient treatment technician.

Divorced, Delanie moved back to Kelso, a year later, she continued her career dancing in Portland for the next four years, while she worked as a receptionist/crisis counselor. She met a "wonderful" man that her children loved, adored and accepted. The only father figure they had ever known.

Suddenly, the relationship and dancing came to an end while the pain was extended long after, as was the confusion of where she was going to find the strength to get through the humbling experiences.

Now, with a whole new perspective on life, men and relationships, single, with very few true friends, her kids and her can only rely on GOD and each other at this time. With new goals, a brighter future, Delanie has returned to her reliable childhood Christ for guidance, strength and show of will.

Dedications

It's peculiar how you guys have affected my life from the depths of my heart, some under the best of light and some not such good light. A couple of you achieved affecting my life doing both.

This dedication is to all the grown ass men who couldn't handle the responsibility that goes along with being a man, and got stuck behaving like little boys. You had a piece of my heart, but never got the best of me. If you liked what you had you should have respected it. Maybe one day you will learn the important difference between quantity and quality. Also, I dedicate to the two females who had me stressing over a man, succeeded in taking my kindness for a weakness.

To all of you who tried to damage my good heart and held me back from success. For everything I never got to say. I dedicate my final words of farewell in love to you. Like it or not my heart my feelings, my emotions are valid, even if I didn't publish this book.

The names are common. Thus, the poems you read may or may not be about you.

Scott, Wynne, David, Jason, Michelle, J., Jaymee, Pam

Thank You

To my God who gave me the strength, will and courage to stand up to everyone in my dedications. For comforting me with reassurance that I am not alone and did not deserve to be disrespected by any of the people I have been from my past in the way that they had. Thank you for guiding me to learn and grow from all of my losses and mistakes.

Thank you Dori, for building my manuscript and having the technical skills that you do, thank God for you.

Thank you IUniverse, for giving me the opportunity to uniquely express the truth of my own demons, in my own way, love, bi-polar or not.

Thank you so much to my true friends and family who have encouraged me not to give up on myself and not doubt my own capabilities.

Thank you Mom and Dad, for forcing me to chase my dreams, accomplish my goals and use my whole potential.

J.C. and Connie it means so much to me that you helped me out in such an important way I appreciate your friendship deeply, thank you for listening to me cry and bitch about these problems you are golden. You never judged me in my craziest states of mind.

Thank you Katie for helping me type the book. Reva, Rushunn, Tyler, Julio, Gail, Dionne, and Justin thank you for standing by my side in sincerity with my best interest at heart.

Dr. Joey for forcing me to see that doing better for myself didn't have to mean finding a better man, even though I was and am worthy of that too.

Thank you Debbie for seeing my heart and encouraging me to reach higher. I love you so much. You're always going to have a piece of my heart forever!

Jason, we really have been through it all, I do and always have loved the deeper you, thank you for helping me grow, I will continue to pray that you do the same.

Thank you Scott and David, for giving me the opportunity to be a great mom to our kids, even though I don't know where you are, we can't find you anywhere.

Thank you Jaymee and the other David, for allowing yourself to be my temporary stepping stones.

Last and most precious my awesome children you are both so understanding and put up with all of the adversities, stayed strong through all the changes, and taught me how to be a stronger woman and mom. Thank you for being you, thank you for being the biggest part of my heart today and for every day that comes in the future.

Morning Glorious

They got lost in a kiss
Swayed by his eyes deep and brown
Unsure of what she found
A man pure and true
Got lost in her eyes
A crystal blue
Swayed by her tender lips
Longing for depth between her hips
Made love, honest yet mild to produce no child
Created a relationship solid as stone
Comfortably, no commitments thrown
Does he love her enough?
Yes or no
She doesn't wander anymore
He wants to give her everything under the sun
Even in spite of, commitment often undone
The marriage in backyard morning becomes a hazy mist
To get lost in another meaningful kiss
Until the moment is met again
They remain just best friends
She dreams of commitment defined
Something real- something satisfied
Both longing for no more illusions
No more confusion
Something they call us
Lets all pray they have a morning so glorious

Crazy Love

You stole my heart once
And won it over twice
Maybe three times
If I remember right
I know how true love
Still flows along
Yet, after her
We just don't get along
How can something so deep
Turn out so wrong
We both know our love was true
Through and through
Looking back again
I remember you my best friend
Maybe time heals along
Maybe I'm all wrong
I have hurt as you as you have hurt me
Is their a remedy?
Make love are feelings I say
May never happen
All I can do is pray
You call me crazy
Some of its true
I agree
Mostly, crazy over you

Lost a Friend

You will catch me if I shall fall
You will answer me if I call
You will brighten the dark that plagues my newly a banded soul
You will be encouragement though all my obstacles
You and all you touch
I assume remaining friends was too much
You my angel sent from above
Gave up-every time things got rough
Enduring constant battles through out life
You carrying us through brighter times
Good for you, scarring three hearts for life
I wasn't going to bear all the strife
You will never lie as taught and told
You only have truth
Harboring to your grave to hold
You want to be there for me
Even when I want to be alone
If you truly wanted me as a friend
It's been unknown
Because, that is just what friends will do
Through it all, always beside you
Were you honestly being a friend?
Your actions showed you wanted it all to end
Now I'm left to mourn the one I befriend
I will often mourn him
Until my life ends

Going Alone

As I sit alone in my own misery
Seeking for that little bit of peace
There are not definite answers
They elude you and me
Unable to comprehend what's been done
Trying to make sense of it
All every day
I take back all that's done wrong
Pray that it's worked out before long
Everyone always abandoned me
Our hearts beat as one, don't you see
I didn't feel you could
I didn't think you would
It's frightening this place
I wander if I could escape
I often express kindness and love
I utter words only in truth
Only to be obscured by you
I have given all that I am
What more do you ask me to do?
I have been honest, faithful, and patient
Kind loving and true
Is there something else
I'm supposed to do

I pray all the time for answers
In hopes my life goes on
The Ache Allows
Death to gaze my heart and beyond
I will not keep living in this chaos
And misery for me to own, alone
I know the lord
Will be faithful
He always answers me
In desperate plea
He sends yet, another angel
To deliver me back
To where I can be free
"No fear my child" he whispers
"You and he were meant to be"
"Let go and let me"
"Have patients in faith and time my child
You once more will be able
To call him, forever mine"

Eternity

Unsure of how much exactly
I have hurt you so
You don't know how deeply
You have stabbed me through
We have both drawn blood
Still longing to love and be together
Internal hearts walls we keep
Things arise and gone wrong
Can be resolved if we choose
Lord knows we love each other true
Neither of us can stand to lose
For what is lost
Can be found
Put strength in your will
Force us to another round
I am patient standing in fiery glass
If it means
You're true at last
However long it may take
Though, its sacrifices we make
For you my true love
Near future or eternity
I will wait

Just Between Me and You

Who am I now? Where do I go from here?

Why is it suddenly there's a lot to fear?

You broke me down and tore me apart

I have nothing for you within my heart

Nowhere to start

I never wanted to be without you

What do we do? Where do we go?

Could we even get back?

What was lost though?

I cry even when I don't want to

I only need emotional respect from you

I started over yet, you are still there

Which means you still care?

So what steps must we take?

To heal each others heartache

Will you keep a part of me?

Or continue holding out on family

That's what we were

Became crazy stir, now all a blur

I never wanted someone, something new

I don't want you

To keep me holding on

Aching my heart black & blue

Are we letting go?

Or are we still one- actually two

Just between me and you

There Has Never Been

There has never been
Anyone who hurts so deep
There has never been
Anyone I miss more when I sleep
There has never been
Anyone I would rather hold close
There has never been
Anyone I have loved the most
There has never been
Anyone to touch every place in my heart
There has never been
Anyone able to tear it apart
There has never been
Anyone so confused
There has never been
Anytime I felt so misused
There has never been
Anyone when things weren't okay
There has never been
Anyone whom so devoted entered my life
There has never been
Anyone who could cut so deep in two
Like a knife
It's all hiding amongst sin
I know because
There has never been

Hearts Desire

I often run to you to watch
What you will do next
Are you ready to love again yet?
At some point I must walk away
But, today is not that day
I have faith in GOD
And continue to pray
You say you want to come to me
That you want to be free within us
Whole heartedly
You want to learn and grow
Be the nick knack to your patty whack
Until we are old
If that day never arrives
I feel expected to live life un alive
It is you who fulfills all my emotions
It is for you I would cross the oceans
I dislike feeling vulnerable or desperate
But what have I done wrong
To keep your heart from loving mine for so long
A lot of it, is your issues I know
I just fear
You'll never let them show

Loves Dying Breath

Gave our hearts completely
Offered it full and true
All that we are we offered to you
Suddenly, loves destiny chilled
What was there?
Now has been killed
Unrequited,
Longed for connection, affection
Always unfulfilled
Sweet pain never truly dies
Even through all rumors and lies
Where is your remorse?
Tears falling free
Show no sorrow deep
Without it we do not heal
Important to us to express how you feel
Otherwise, in loves dying breath
Our hearts ache
Reach their dawning death

Seven Sinful

You lash out at me
With anger and SCORN
Simply doesn't hurt anymore
I let go and let God carry out the deed
You can try to take the world
But you won't succeed
You can leave me too
But, it is your life in utter sin
Didn't they tell you, you have
A short life to live oh' from your friends
I have nothing to give
Well in time you'll see I'm just fine
For the GREED you soak alive
Is causing you to die
There is no way you can say I didn't care
I put in many prayer
Let your own ENVY feed your power
Your obsessions even in loyalty are devoured
Taking care of only yourself through GLUTTNEY

Those things you speak of
Thy are not me
We occasionally basked in SLOTH
Though now, it's only you alone with what
You have bought
I'm sad your self esteem is so low
That PRIDE gave option
For you to let good go
Messing with my intelligence
Using that same pride and LUST
That thing that helped bring us together
Now broke free from us
I'm okay now you see
The WRATH is not on me
If I did so much wrong
It seems defiantly odd
By the time your sorry's report to God
One of us
Will already be gone

You

You center of my universe
You unworthy of every verse
You abomination to me
Your little girl
No longer my hero
Not a diamond not a pearl
You trapped within your own box
You want out
Like chicken pen cocks
You had one family
Left me behind
You will see
You shut up!
You never mind
You special to only a few
You a coward and weak
Huh……
Who knew?
By Iesha

All Those Times

All those stories, all those lies
All those times you made me cry
I have wondered once and worried twice
Even flipped out a few times
All the shit you put me through
And you claim I hurt you?
All those times I waited up
I'm done, you're out of luck
All those times, excuses
Such a bore
I'm over it, run back to your whore
All those times, your to busy
Get over yourself; I don't need you for me
All the emotional abuse
Find someone else to put up with you
All the tears, all the pain
I don't deserve this, not again
All those times
You called it love
How could a smart girl be so dumb?
All those times
I couldn't move on
I have wised up
You turn to cry
I'm gone!!!

Home Wrecker

It's time for you wake up call
He is not attracted to you at all
You knowingly slipped between
To get involved
You kyped his heart
From two girls
Without care you stumble and stall
You try to blame me
Talk about me being crazy
You're no friendly daisy
You know who I am?
No you don't-you asked for my help
I lent my hand
Then you turn to say my kindness is weak
He's not off the hook
Though, I trust you're the home wreaking freak
Selfish without further ado
The damage comes back to you
Your self esteem is in the dumps
He just used you, like your others
For lonely day humps
You're desperate to take attention from anybody
No matter the age of the kids or bond in the family
Your twisted attraction and desire
Proved I was true and you the LIAR!

Sad and scary, my sloppy seconds

Pumps you with adrenaline

Worse, he loved me but because of you

He will never know what could have been

Funny, you convinced yourself

It was about love

Yet, even without me

He places no one above

Your deluded within yourself

My advice bitch-seek professional help

Your behavior is disgusting

You'll only get what you bring

Have pity on your unpleasing heart

Somewhere you should start

You wonder why you don't sleep well at night

All forsaken pain you brought

While I comfort my girls assuring them

Every things alright

Take your own jealousy and misdirected anger I guess

Live in your own emotional filthy mess

I care about him and need him happy

Give him the child you kept

Set his heart free

Dose it not bother you

Its me-he cry's I love you too

I know you don't care haven't from the start

Yet, it was my family

You tore apart

Fuck You Crack Head

Fuck you for not listening to what's left to say
Fuck you for being greedy every single day
I'm not your fucking friend but you are my fucking foe
Fuck you, all your drama, I let go, fucking hoe
Fuck you; you can think what you want
Fuck you, your still a cunt
Fuck you, I never hated anyone before
Fuck you, home wrecker your worse than a whore
Fuck you, for thinking I was weak
Bow down bitch, lick my fucking feet
Fuck you, that I was ever kind
Fuck you; it still blows my fucking mind
Fuck you and how you were raised
The only honor you receive is in the devils eyes praised
Fuck you, for making me literally ill
Fuck you, you're such a pill
Fuck you, being that ugly takes skill
Fuck you for thinking you were worthy of any piece of my heart
Fucking bitch I'm glad your marriage and family fell apart
Nasty, dirty, fucking bitch, blowing anyone for your next hit
Fuck you for not letting her father know
Fuck you for letting your little girl go

Over some fucking blow

Fuck you, and the years he has been denied

Fucking dumb ass hoe-lied

Fuck you, for causing so many to cry

Fuck you for thinking you had power in all of this

Fucking egotistical bitch

I expect you realize this poem is a diss

Fucking crack head I hate you for smothering his pain underneath

I wish I could stop your privilege to breath

You are a fucked up mom

And fucked over her blood dad

Now you're all alone….aaaw….too fucking bad

You call me crazy like I am inconvenient to your world

Fuck you….stupid girl

Still puffin your fucking pipe

That's right; she probably has a better life

Fuck you, for hurting so many without care

No one likes you,

My heart dose not fucking spare

Fuck you, I wish you dead

Fuck you fucking crack head

Interrupted Love

You fucking bitch I hate your guts
It's no one else's fault but your own
You were a slut
You expected him to feel sorry for you
You fucking borderline, narcissistic bitch
Get over yourself, look for a clue
You made your decisions
That mad a lot mad
Fucking whore
Should've thought about the consequences at hand
Now he fears you
Won't stand up and be a man
Also, because of you it's me
He doesn't understand
You are vainglory in what you have caused
Unfortunately-on judgment day
I wish your entry to be paused
That's what you have done to us
You fucking Huss
I wish upon you
That you eat satins toe jam
Then he bends you over
And fucks you in your punan
You interrupted a good thing

You wouldn't understand

You pawned your wedding ring

If I didn't have children of my own

I'd kick your sleazy ass

Wait! On 2nd thought

I won't stupe down to your level

Miss 5th class

We may end because of you

And

I'll meet you in hell

For all my sinister thoughts

Of killing you too

You are the most greedy

Bitch I'd ever met

It aint over yet

The only man I loved true

I'm gonna lose him

Because I have no respect for you

Would you be there for him if I were gone?

No-I know that and he will before long

You were never worthy of him at all

I hope you realize it's true

And it makes you ball

Ya see, he's figuring your deceitful game

Along the way

You need to know

I'm a better woman than you

So with me his heart will always stay

Fuck You Punk

Fuck you punk for being irate
Fuck you for making me experience hate
Fuck you mutha fucker you determined your own fate
Fuck the fact there is no we
Fuck the future we will never see
Fuck our precious past and its memories
Fuck you and what you could never be
Fuck your damn hoe and jiggaboo
Fuck pain harbored inside too
Just as well, fuck the chance you blew
Fuck the trust that wasn't given back
Fuck the happiness you now lack
Fuck the vicious bitch who threw us off track
Fuck the sex that shit was wack
Fuck you I never want you back
I'm glad for the end of all that
Fuck when you follow what you were taught,
The greed, insensitivity, and bullshit you sought
Fuck you-you are not worth my hope
Fuck you-and your narrow minded scope
So-Fuck us Both-No-Not me just you
You're a sluggish kind of slime-Set me free
I'm so fucking relieved I'm no longer with you

What? The truth carved in
Fuck you and your sin
Fuck the ulcers-they made me so thin
You're fucking lazy-So what if I'm crazy
You would be to put on the edge
Fuck you and the scar on your head
Fuck the power trip you've been on
Fuck Mick Nasty's, yard sale, granny thong
Fuck you pushing me to the brink
I'm ignorant-That's what you think!?
Smart enough to run from you
You were following me for a minute
That fucking blew
Fuck you and all your cheap thrills
Fuck you and your pills
Fuck you and the misery with
You I had to live
Fuck everything you didn't say
But hid
Fuck you because you were all we lived for
Fuck you punk never again-No MORE!

Fuck you for keeping me from being me

Fuck you-I Didn't Need Your Sympathy

Fuck you-my kid's hearts poisoned a sickened

I'm keeping them safe from you-I'm insisted

So now-I'm selfish committed

Fuck you-because you'll never admit

Fuck all your words that rot away

Fuck you-is pretty much all I want to say

Fuck you for not caring one bit

Fuck you we quit

Fuck you for nothings the same

And nothing changes

Fuck you-now we get to be alone

Fuck you, my lyrics, and this poem

Fuck you now that you're gone

I can finally breathe

Not to mention get some fucking sleep

I have every right to speak

I don't know when to shut up

Fuck you-fucking punk

Oh no now you know how my heart bleeds

You weren't man enough to meet my needs

Fuck you-bothered by a phone call

Fuck you-you are a piece of shit that's all!

Thought 2 Consider

My father figure
Even after the break up
You insisted on a family picture
You try to blame my mom
It was your emotions that
Blew up like a bomb
My heart is half full
Yours remains half empty
I can't believe you left me
Damn, that hurts
You once made me smile and laugh
Too bad now, it's all in the past
As time goes by
I still don't understand reasons
You and the rest wanted me to cry
My mom tried as hard as she could
Though, she stood up for herself
Like she should
She was only protecting my heart
Because she knew
You guys were falling apart
You told me you would never leave
Now,
Just another man
I obviously can't believe

Thought II Consider

As we all sit in the misery
She's casting shadows with smiles
Because she knows we could never be
I'm disappointed in you
You let her win
I dream all the time
What could have been
Procrastinating on us
When you already know
Moms no "huss"
Though I find Michelle a stupid hoe
I think everyone should know
It really is he fault
She put our family at halt
Her life goes on
My family is still gone

She let her blood get so hurt at seven
Man she may not make it to heaven
Little girl-I don't blame you
His plan was to add you to our
Family a few
I'm angry most of all
Because now I don't have a daddy to call
You promised to keep in touch
I figured you wouldn't on a hunch
My young life's journey continues on
No one should blame my mom
She should be praised
For staying strong
My hearts always been with you
While you battered mine black & blue
Something to give some thought
You deserve your daughter how you have sought
But we didn't deserve the pain you brought
Something else to consider too
It's not fair
Only me continuing to long and love you

By Iesha

The Bad Potion

If I could do it all over
I'd choose you
to be my daddy once more
even if I lost you again
it's worth all the tears
in the world puddled to heaven
you were my sunshine
now, my sky's are gray
I loved you and bonded to you
because you new how to play
my unhappiness away
I was proud to be your little girl
sometimes we argued
but you were always my whole world
you treated me as your own
though your time with me
seemed to have got cut short
my heart is completely crushed
but mama says nothing loved is ever lost
and you are loved so much
I remember our trip to the ocean
the one you must have forgot
when you drank the bad potion
I want to see you Jason
it's been seven years
be careful when you drink the bad potion
it will keep you from
the ones you hold dear
I think the bad potion was in your beer.

Personal from Jessica to Jason

Good Ol' Days

What is it that is left?

I said last night

As I dreamt

You held me tight once again

Everything felt right

Was this our last night?

After everything that we have been through

I wonder if it's still you.

Still to this day

We can get lost in each others eyes

With that sexy gaze

Did we still have something?

Nah, it was just a dream

Memorizing the good ol' days

Letting Go

I have let go and so have you
You had to do what you had to
So here it is finally the end
I'll always remember you as my old friend
What has been done to my kid's finesse?
Is only our business
We happen to be doing great
So, keep your head up, please don't hesitate
For, I hope you find your own piece of mind
Thank you, for letting me go
We discovered a beautiful life
That we otherwise wouldn't know
It's all been a blessing in disguise
Your unworthiness, I will not patronize
You will get to that far away place
it is within your soul
Keep it embraced
Once you finally find it, you will know
I pray you won't ever let it go
It's deep within your soul
I know because
That's where I found diamonds and gold
Live your life strictly for you
And never forget
Who always loved you?

Understanding

Go ahead and wait for your world to change
The thought alone is deranged
Created sacrifice in letting me go
The only difference it makes to you
Is that im better off you should know
Unsure of why I trusted in giving you another turn
I fell for your game
Played with fire, and again, got burned
Your world turned upside down and twisted
I flipped mine around – now, I am found
Deep within my soul
I am finally whole
Like a caged bird let loose to fly
The puzzle fell apart
I leave the broken pieces behind
I am no longer misunderstood
I finally get what it means to be treated good
At the end of us, I had heard but had never seen
It is no longer a mystery

Appeasing Hearts

Just when I thought there were
No more tears to cry
I had laid down to realize it's all a lie
I still hurt deep inside
I say I don't because
True feelings I try to hide
No matter where I run near or far
When I look deep into my heart
There you are
Where you will always remain
Even though we will never be together again
I have to put you to rest
As you figure out what it is that you need to know
No matter how hard I try
I can't ever fully let go
Not because I don't want to
It's because the Lord said my heart
Was supposed to belong to you
I would deny that if I could
I have like I should
Even you can't deny
There are many more tears to cry
Getting over each other isn't easy
Especially when our hearts
Together are so appeasing

Falling Back

Who are you leaving us to fend alone
It is with grace
I pull out immense thorn
No one can hold me back
I'll take off with courage
Like troops in attack
You weren't man enough
To hold me down
I can stand on my own two feet for many rounds
You may push us aside
Yet, the wind is where we ride
Not a single soul with whom we rely
Based all on one persons lie
We still have each other though
More peaceful than you will ever know
You wished me weak
Though true meaning of existence
We will continue to seek
No! You may not hold onto my heart
I'll reserve it for someone deserving
A fresh start
You leave me and my girls alone now
I will make it up to them somehow
You'll have your chance in heaven
You can kiss there toes and cry as you bow
Because all three of us fall way back from you now

Always Love Her

What is she doing?
Does her mom realize who she is screwing?
I shouldn't have let her go
Now, I will never know
I am so lost don't know how to be found
I love here I would tell the whole world
All the way around
She deserves diamonds, taken to see things
And go places that may occur
Her mom is a bitch though
Because I couldn't ever control her
She deserves the best
I have lost her, forget the rest
Living in the same city
I miss her she's so gentle and pretty
I don't have to buy her a Cadillac or Ferrari
All I really want her to know is "I am sorry"
Her and her brother deserve so much better
I wish them good
She could comfort me like no other
Not having her is worse than the pain
In the passing of my grandma, dad and brother
I could easily make everything alright
But what if I fail? I think I might
One day I planned our future
The next I left her alone
Fought my friends - stitches and sutchers
I can't be with her or let her go
I will always love her she needs to know
I love her the most and always will
With out her my life is not filled

In honor of Jason to Taylor

Has Been

As we wait for the madness
To surpass
We realize it just doesn't
Its always going to last
Letting go is never
An easy task
Respecting someone else's heart
Isn't either when, has to be asked
So now we go
And here we are gone
Left alone, to miss our sacred bond
Moved on, yes you know
No one can touch what we had though
No more tears left to cry
Only loving memories
We try to hide
Sometimes we flash a smile
When we don't get to hold
You for that little while
Because it's more peaceful than
Explaining why we are sad
Besides, it is easier for the kids
To pretend they still have a dad
Maybe one day you will have time to put in
Until then
You are just another has been

I Miss Daddy

Daddy's Love Cuts Deep

I know you love him
But, chances of being together are very slim
The scars are to many
Not sparing our hearts are the same
As not sparing a penny
Since he cant put you first the
Outcome is the worst
We all have lost a dear friend
Remember mommy's love never ends
He is not close to valuable of what you are worth
To mommy you will always come first
I am always here my darlings have no fear
I often pray only my love is enough
Somehow, suck it up girls get tough
I understand it was your first daddy love
Im sorry you got cut
Feel it in my hug
Im truly sorry for all of that
Sometimes we love but don't always get it back
It's a lesson learned you can give all you have
By chance, it may not be returned
Please don't give up, love exist still
Move forward
Pull the strength from your will
Together we can find that faith leap
Even though daddy's love cuts so deep.

Mommy Needs You Too

Mommy tries as hard as she can

Why are you angry with me

It's not fair- I don't understand

I was only standing up for myself

Even if it meant

Living with out money and wealth

More importantly my sanity and health

He was disrespectful to me

I needed to set an example of it being a possibility

I won't let my girls grow up to think its okay to be treated like that

It easily could have been - a matter of fact

I value your love so much more

Giving up my lover, and so what?

We live financially poor

Please don't allow yourself to blame me

He has issues, we set him free

We are richer in our hearts

Don't let this tear us apart

This is not all because of me

I did things wrong

But nothing close to his mistrust

Please believe

Sure I treated him bad

After he hurt my girls and made you sad

I didn't start this whole thing

Except the paternity and the glorious truth

It was supposed to bring

So much for lending my hand

We got used and then

We were all banned

Exposed

Use my kids against you?

No! I did not

You're the one crawling back to me

Oh wait" you must have forgot

Telling our friends things that are not true

Keep lying to yourself

Remember, I left you

I'll never forget how you came to me that day

Sleep with me Delanie, please I pray

Practically in tears

Promising to love me and the girls

for the rest of your years

I felt sorry for you and so I did

That's when you confessed

You thought Michelle was a bitch

You wish you had never met

Yeah I believe that was your wish.

If she hadn't entered our life

Everything would be alright

Your right and I am wrong

All I heard for five weeks long

Lie to yourself and anyone else that you want

I state the facts true and blunt

In any stricken pose

For now, the truth is exposed

Emotionally Retarded

Let me string myself along

Making promises for your own convenience

It's all so wrong

You always say you'll call

But never do when you say

Feels like you want me to fall

Little boy games

Dirty liar shames

You are old enough to know

Not wise enough to let it show

Go ahead,

Run with the crowd

Take your pride

Make us all proud

Not caring for any feeling except your own

Saying one thing but doing another

Okay you had me torn

Not my problem anymore

You are so emotionally retarded

Laid to rest,

My dearly departed

Love Sober

Once again dark souls

Twisted and intertwined

Lost again I whine

When I die will he care?

Though it doesn't matter

Love spreads everywhere

Delicate touches amongst my skin

Loving him back feels like sin

When emptiness finds my heart

Too many times over

I wish to never meet with him again

Remain love sober

I cherish time shared

Feels like other things important spared

When no one feels a word said

I remember, it's all in my head

Ha! So that's what he says

Never feeling true to the artery

It doesn't matter

I live my life for me

One day – love drunk cornered

Will someday be true love sober?

At Ease

Restful and at ease
I understand the peace
Aura's shining
Angel's spirits combining
Prayed for emotional growth
When does it come though?
Unanswered it's all the same
Forever, has no shame
It embraces your body, mind, and soul
It makes you believe you are
The other half to the whole
If it is true you will be restful and at ease
You will understand the peace
When friends and lover's
Aura's are shining
When angel's spirits
Are forever combining

To be published in "Immortal Verses Dec. 2009"
By the International Library of Poetry.

Angel's Hearts Kidnapped

My two angels that I have
I'm sorry your hearts were kidnapped
Iesha my boo and Jessica my bug
Too both of you, I cherish every hug
I'm sorry they couldn't see
Our love as a priority
They were all unworthy
Of how special you are
They didn't love you like I
My shining stars
And no, the world doesn't
Revolve around us
What we deserve versus
What we got was unjust

There is no explanation or excuses

For what they have done

That's the reason

I call them out….

Then they run

They don't know how to take responsibility

Or even say sorry

So we leave

Not caring for your feelings is unacceptable

Don't worry my angel's

GOD says our hearts are perishable

I'm careful not to let

This ever happen again

But you really need to let go

Though your love never has to end

The pain will be zapped

Thus, GOD and I can

Rescue your hearts from being kidnapped

Love,
Mommy

The Drawing Board

Back to the drawing board I go
Still seeking answers to my restless soul
You are my ex-girlfriend "I said"
Though we can still go to bed
I want to love you to
But I am scared of you
I have learned what your love
Can cause
Builds sky high walls
Brings my emotions to a pause
I need you in my life more than you know
Though I refuse to
Get or give closure
I don't want to let you go
No matter who is by my side
You're always in my heart
I can't honestly deny
I can't be with you
I don't trust myself too
You are at the bottom of every bottle though
There is so much pain behind the entertainment
Now everyone knows
You speak for me
As though you are my entity
So, maybe you are
I just don't see that far - In Honor of Jason to his true love

Dormant Emotions

I love your potential

But it's not enough

I will not bet my life on it

Alone for us

One day I dream it steadfast

All together at last

The immortal part of our bodies

Blended whole

Separated temporarily

Yet, no matter where in the world

We are frequently united souls

Not a single human can snatch

What GOD has planned

In the Lords palms

Is where true lover's hearts land

You may lay your passions dormant

Withdrawal them and lie

Need I remind you

The sincerity of your potential

Is in the sight

Of the holy spirits eye?

To be published in Favorite Memories

By Noble House April 2009

Once In a While

Once in a while
You will find a friend
Whose determination
Never ends
You'll find someone too
Who wants to understand you?
Near or far
They will love every piece
Of who you are
When you are sad
Or want to be left alone
It's you they want to hold
Once in a while
Just to see this person
You would walk miles
No matter how much you take
They will always give
This is how your friend lives
Give or take
This friend cannot be replaced
Every once in a while
You are blessed
With a friend who is your smile.

Intellect

Physically on earth we met
Who loved more, we bet?
Neither the same
None with no shame
Open we were to everyone
Nothing was stopping us
Under the moon or the sun
Ignited a fiery blaze
Wind blew and we
Were lost for days
Yet, we did not burn
We still love
But there's nowhere to turn
Cognitively, I cannot tell
Emotionally, I know
No one can take true love to hell
Standing strong amongst
Angelic spirits on earth today
Together forever
In your arms or miles away
In person
We are none to reject
It's a force beyond
Our intellect

My Man Restless

A friend I cherish and love

I prayed for him everyday

To the good lord above

Asked him to bless me

With happiness and laughter

Then, my life wouldn't be such a disaster

I do love him I must admit

Putting so many hearts on the line is a huge risk

True love is hard to find

Good love is easy

With tools, experience and design

My mind and schedule chaotic, his schedule tight

I speak of him often throughout the day

And dream of him into the night

His smile brightens my day

Sometimes I feel so blessed

I just don't know what to say

No matter what I think I feel

I need a relationship real

All I ever asked for is one true lover friend
No options for a relationship to end
When I fall he will help me stand
Absolutely cares about me
Communicates- takes responsibility
Agrees to disagree
Life is so hard alone
So many obstacles
With a friend like him
I might buy into believing in miracles
After the work weak and kids in school
Hanging with him just seems pretty cool
Whenever, wherever, when down on my luck
Spending time with him
Seems like the world doesn't suck

My Man Restless continued……

I really do love him so
He has always been my heart
I don't want to let go
Will he wait for me till im ready or better?
Will he hate me after this letter?
He has had time plus contact to heal
I have had only months
Don't know what I deeply feel
I know my aim is true
What I don't know is
Can a heart beat forever loving?
After one love was beaten black and blue
Torn an slashed in more pieces than two
All I ever wanted in my forever friend
I might have found
But, what if it's just a rebound?

I tell him to take it slow

Where we end up no one knows

Is it really fair if one of us has more to share?

Im in love with all the ideas he has

Living it up and letting go of the past

I love when he holds me

It sets that much more of my darkened spirit free

Something tells me GOD is not done

He has much more work to do

In rebuilding my heart new

Even though I mean it

When I say I love you

I think he may not be worthy

Of spiritually holding my hand

Is he emotionally, mentally, strong enough to be my man

For now, my man is so restless

What does he have to say now?

Then I have left him breathless

You're the One

You feel my heart with love
You are my only sweet
You make my heart feel it's beat
You are my true oasis
You are my strength
When Im cornered into weak places
When it's all said and done
You are my love, the only one
You are the one for my setting suns
You are the one for shooting paintball guns
You are the one I'd want to embrace in arm
You are the one whom I rely on in harm
When life is said and done
My true love- you are the one
You inspire my soul to sing
You and I sharing all the diversities life brings
The one to share tears when I am sad
The one to laugh with when I am glad
When all is said and done
I know in my heart
Mommy - you are the one
Love, Your Daughters

I See Through Him Mama

He pecks your check

Though it seems sweet

Attempting to make your heart

Skip another beat

He grabs your hip

I watch you bite your lip

Trying to fight it you are no good at hiding it

Mom, I don't get it I don't seem to understand

You know he's no longer a good man

He often skips out on you causing tears

Don't think I don't hear you crying

He doesn't care anymore and otherwise he wouldn't be lying

Also, if you don't think you can do better

Mama, look around

Everyone I know says you the hottest in town

I have courage from you

I let him go and know you can too

Have faith and patience

You will find the right one

Someone prideful in calling you Hon

Don't worry you pretty little face

The Lord in time will send

Him to fill you up

In that special place.

By, Iesha

Mocked One More Time too Many

The pathway to your feelings Is all too numb
When I approach you with mine
You call the scenario dumb
I reach for you, I really do
Every time I do- I get screwed
You say you care about what is inside
Though, when it's actually in the open
You run and hide
Little spirit child, oh so blue
I'm sorry for the things you go through
There is nothing wrong with the way I talk
Perhaps the problem lye's in the way you mock
Not my problem you have skills unlearned
Holding onto me
Keeps your hopes up like you yearned
Emotionally, uncommitted this far
Will never find honest meaning
Consumed within your heart
Sorrow to say
I gave up on you sociopath
You have mocked me wrong
For the last time, yesterday
You give the child away
For a hustle on a dollar, dime, or penny
The girls and I have now
Been mocked one more time too many.

If Only My Memory Could

Insensitivity is where your heart is stale

Drinking and popping pills until you are pale

A turn off to someone

Who once adored and cared for you true

Until she realized she wasn't the problem

It was you

You made her feel as though she were Satan's spawn

Until the Lord showed her, that's wrong

It was you all along

Spears, knives, and crosses

What little memories were shared?

Now, chalked up as losses

It's not like you went out of your way to show her you loved her everyday

In fact, verbally abusive, in secret belittled her every single day

That's not right, and you said this wrong

Here, let me get my violin I'll play you a fucking song

Hero and victim, that's what you are right

BE BOTH

I give up the fight

I know now I can't win

You're unwilling to break through

Make change on selfish sin

You want me to believe that I'm no good

Well, I never met you before

If only my memory could

State Of Mind

State of mind
Numbed to hide
Rescue this
Pissen and moaning
Like a little bitch
Anger and destruction
Under the influence
Emotionally cannot function
Make a buck
Violate a girl
Than tell her to get fucked
Rage is the name of your heart
When your sober we will never part
Drink a fifth sell a sack
Same little boy, no, I don't want you back
Diss family for your friends
It's a state of mind cycle with you, it never ends
Poppin pills cuz you're sick
Not physically
But in that heart of your that is
Only connected to your dick
Like a little bitch
Pissen and moaning
Rescue this
Numbed to hide
State of mind

Conjuring Inside

Conjuring inside
Pressures I hide
One tear falls from my eye
Brush it away
Just as you shewed
My emotions the other day
You mean nothing to me anymore
I tell myself that open into truths door
The pressures keep building
Until the tears pour, im fighting them back
When I admit my feelings I get attacked
It's not that you don't care at all
Inside you too
Pain, slithers and crawls
Left alone in the midst of the ride
Pressures I hide
Conjuring inside

Suffering

Check to pay the bill
Bill to cash the check
Two little girls, raising alone
What the heck?
What happened to child support?
Off the hook
Without even showing up to court
One in prison
The other screwed in the head
Both in my eyes financially dead
Aren't they supposed to help?
With the babies they made
Emotionally nonexistent
Physically, affectionately resistant
Not a single soul they truly rely
I wont give up – always another try
They know this, I see it in there eyes

Punished for trusting another and beyond

I just need my children happy

That's where they belong

So much pressure to be the hero

When every single guy begins and ends

With a big fat zero

Lord, peace, and harmony

Please GOD I beg

Don't forget about my children or even me

You know its time to pay too

Because so many years I have paid my due's

Now I realize I need some help

I can't do this alone

No more broken glass

Or bruises from the stone

Lord, please send cash

No one to reach out to

Not even by phone

Alcohol

Berry grey goose

Dancing and laughing

Cutting me loose

Tequila sunrise by the sea

Maken me believe

I'm capable of every fantasy

X-rated fusion a treasured liquor store find

Taking your time

While you alter my mind

Mixing you with energy

So we don't seem to numb

Sometimes a favorite

Redbull and rum

You let me tell the story

How I think it should be told

Celtic crossing

One bottle down- the next one sold

Any kind of whiskey

Sets my tongue free

Telling truths about all the lies

Tequila Spider bite pulled over charged with D.U.I.

How many shots, would you like?

Brandy, seduce me for an escape

Combined ties rape my pain away

We are now barflies

And you, you say you'll give me anything

If I make you my next of kin

Hmmm… I believe your name is gin

Jagger blaster, ran out of money faster

It's all about alcohol and having a good time

Right? And never tired of the corny lines?

Oh we're having fun now until the morning realizing the head you got or gave was
with a fat cow.

When feeling to real gets near

Gambling cash away

Make it cheap convenient store beer.

Circling around to the top we can do it again this year

Problem Child

Problem child to society

Close to GOD, yet, still un-mighty

Ruled by city officials

Go ahead pull me over

As long as I still know who worked hard

To push my own wheels

Government says I can't

Though I WILL

I'm me over and over still

Take my drivers license away

I'm still great full for everything I have today

Although some not important

Looking to my heart as I pray

Keep trying never knock me down

Bad luck caught me

Whatever, within my soul I'm sound

Money and greed – greed and money

Makes you all happy

While I'm content

Just calling my children honey

Trying to take what I brought to life

No, they don't have a daddy

And no, I'm not a wife

So, my head is still above water

I'm not going to drowned

The pavement man made,

Hurts when my feet hit the ground

Stopping at nothing to keep what is mine

Won't except you hassling me

Let me be, I'm just fucking fine

Keep forcing your rules and regulations upon me

I'll forever remain

Problem child to your society

Thank Jesus

Standing so strong

Feeling so weak

Begging for answers

Why do you hand these things to me?

Lord,

I only live to be mild and meek

Some pressures overwhelmingly big

I think stronger

As I smoke another cig.

Everything I took from the world

But couldn't keep

I owe it back

Repenting

I do weep

Greatly extended inward with sorrow

I lend my heart to anyone

In need, if they may barrow

I'll carry through

Though I'm so angry at those

In vain of you

Claim you to be there savior

All the while

Hiding demons and devilish behavior

How many more dollars

Can they rake in?

The interpretation of your word is so mistaken

Lord, I'm calling on you, show me safety

In fulfilling your tasks

Jesus, hear my prayers is all I ask

Because I cry when I'm torn

Though because of you

I'm never left alone

A New Friend

I give such gratitude

For your caring attitude

An a banded soul

Gives grace for another

To mend whole

It is unknown what's left behind

Must be shown

What is broken in me

Is out of my control

Strife always takes a toll

What I say is lost

You say is found

Am I ready to go another round?

Yet, who is glory in all of this

You who makes me giggle so childish

Is it the one above?

Who finds only loyalty

In his creation of love

Weather it's a friend or more

Someone true

Must not be ignored

New friend, for your caring attitude

I give my gratitude.

Palm Tree

Like a palm tree on
An exotic beach
Often I fall out of reach
Like a palm tree on a summer's day
Heavens look upon me
Soaking my heart up as I pray
Like a palm tree in a tropical storm
I stand tall and proud
Yet, so torn
Like a palm tree my limbs do dance
Life always gives me another chance
Like a palm tree
Wind blows past, instead of through me
Embraces my spirit ever so free
Like a palm tree
I often stand alone
My choice, taking on the unknown
Like a palm tree
Full of beauty and grace
My aura can never be stopped
And my heart can never be replaced

Fact or Fiction

Close my eyes to dream
Yet, it's a scary mystery that I see
It's a haunting memory in the dark hour
I have no control, and lost all power
Meant to see positively
Forces blew me down evidently
Murder invited me the next day
Homicide, seemed okay
Death's wish by gaze
Peeked depths into my soul
The angel's stopped me though
"It's not worth it" I was told
Only to have it reoccur again
Waking up longing to repent
No longer encased
In cold steel of my fear
I prayed the demon away
And began a happy new year

Fuck You Some More

Fuck the day you asked me to be yours

Fuck your ex and your new whores

Fuck the years I devoted

You're a liar

Okay, so it's been noted

Fuck you and her lies

I don't even care about the reasons why

Fuck you and the shit you often try

Fuck everything you ever said

Fuck the day we decided to go to bed

Fuck your ego head trip, oh' it's on

Fuck the snatch where your dick has gone

Tired of excuses and lie's

Today I wish you fucking died

That's right my love belongs to someone else

That should make it pretty easy

For you to go fuck yourself

I'm the one that cut your nuts loose from the jar

So fuck you for fucking me over on my repossessed car
You don't fucking care you still have your stupid pick up truck
So, fuck you, me and my fucked up luck
Amanda was right I shouldn't have invested a buck
Fuck you for me ever trusting you
Fuck you and your pussy ass spoiled moods
I hope you fucking cry for making my kids sob
Fuck your pot, materialistics, and your job
Your mind is so twisted and fucking bent
You thought people would actually believe
I didn't pitch in, buying your toys, and paying the rent
Fuck you and your lack of class
Fuck you punk –
I remember all those times I took care of your ass
Fuck you for not appreciating me but you do it for that whore
Damn it, fuck you some more

Block It Out

Emotions strolling about
Block it out
There is nothing left that I can do
Accept you, for you
Desired property
For a future around you no doubt
Block it out
Continue moving forward
Because things you say are obscured
Can't have my way and I do pout
Block it out
Nothing personal I know
Praying daily your emotions will flow
My love, my life, my route
Interrupted,
Block it out

Your Selfish Heart

The more I tried to be
What you wanted me to be
When I looked into your eyes
I saw the least of me
No matter what good I did
You would always find the unpleased
Constantly tearing me down
And picking me apart
Not knowing how to respect my loving heart
You stay mad because I'm the best you ever had
Knowing your selfish heart
Wasn't supposed to cause all this sad
Your selfish heart just keeps getting its way
Thus, my selfish heart is over yours today.

My Selfish Heart

You need me
Though I'm not there
I want you to love me
Yet, I really don't care
I need someone to know me
Care and understand all
Aspects of me
Allow me to act selfishly
I don't reciprocate
What you want or need
I gave my heart to someone
Else long ago already
You can not capture or keep it
I cry because I know
I am wrong though
I'm really not sympathetic one bit
Because I want what I want
Pure and blunt
Please don't ask anything of me
You will only cause me to be angry
I must do to someone what he has done to me
I will never give into you
Never any commitments
Not for any one man or even two
I will not and do not want to love you

How long has it been?

My first holiday without him
For thanksgiving
I will have turkey with my tears
I believe it's been close to seven years
For Christmas
I will top and string the tree
Carve the turkey
Have a second plate,
I'll do all of this, with a side helping of hate
For Easter Sunday I will pray to GOD
I'm really over the pain
"Today is the day, please Lord I pray"
Halloween has come and gone
He was busy for the birthday, all along
Summer was always fine
All the laughter, fun, and good times
I remember sharing when he was mine
Now, it's a handful of other men
Who want, wait, and stand in line
Though I will never spare my heart
At a drop of a dime
Although I'm forgiven for
All my hate and sin
I still feel the burden
How long does it take?
How long has it been?

He Doesn't Love Me Anymore

He doesn't love me anymore
The agony of it all
How is it? That I long for more
All the demons and skeletons kept hid
But, I still know you did
Love me once upon a time
No longer, never again
I write all of it out in rhyme
I can tell by the cruel words he'll say
All the love he had
Flipped to hate
How that happened
Is beyond control of GOD and me
Besides finally giving up
And setting my heart free
Sometimes I wear his sweatshirt that was lent
I shed a tear because I can smell his scent
If I told him he'd tell me to get bent
Still, my heart is forever sore
Because he doesn't love me anymore

We Were Almost

I was all the heart
You were all the mind
Taking it back to the beginning
Just look- if we rewind
I still have my heart but lost my mind
What I saw in you then
I now can't seem to find
You have your mind but lost your heart
If you were to look for it
You wouldn't know where to start
We were unstoppable
Breaking up was not possible
Ha, your fine without
What you once had
That's too bad
We were almost
Sad you find it convenient to boast
Over my heart
Once your servant and host
Too bad
We were almost

A Mirage

Some things matter
And others don't
Some friends will be there
And others just won't
I saw an angel in my
Sleep yesterday
It told me to tell you
I love you
And walk away

Fair Lady

I view a young lady
Growing up so fair
Even when she does wrong
Look for negativity
It's just not there
Mind and immaturity
Somewhat raped
Though her soul
Remains perfectly heart shaped
Spiritually powerful and strong
Then any has seen before
If you'd like to meet true beauty
I introduce Iesha
No need to look anymore
Always real never shady
I love her dearly
She is my fair lady
In honor of Iesha
Love,
Mommy

Growing Up

Little girl wonderful and mine

If she disagrees she will decline

Personality bold

Her innocence

I'd like to capture and hold

Intellectually divine

She'll test any adult to walk

Her fine lines

Proud of whom she is

Insecure about happiness and bliss

Reaches out when necessary

Clings on when

Pressured by something too scary

Smile that can light up any room

Enjoying her journey as she blossoms and blooms

Loves new toys

Curious about discovering boys

Mom is afraid

What her beauty may do

That sad day

She learns she has the power and strength

To break his heart in two

In honor of Jessica

Love,

Mommy

Mystery Child

Mystery child!
Holding many secrets and truths
Within your heart
Too be forever filed
Pretty girl
When he knew
You became his world
Weather you realize it or not
You are his everything
You are all he's got
And that's a lot
Mystery child
He wants to be the best of you
He holds you deep
In his loyal heart
Pure and true
In honor of Taylor

Take Your Time

You need your time

You need your space….. fine

Deal with the pain

And later when I'm not there

You will have yourself to thank

The love I was willing to give

You can't replace

Nor' can you find a trace

Always when I needed you the most

Tearing me down

And then you boast

In the aggressive game of love

Who is the contestant? Who is the host?

No one can tell, no one wins

Not communicating

Is where love ends and pain begins

Trouble in paradise

Because you never learned to listen

It is okay, my heart even alone

Stands strong and glistens

GOD, my girls, all of me

Just fine

So have your space

And please take your fucking time

Loves Teacher

Dutiful child
Constraining the wild
Anxiety ridden
Comforting tears hidden
Beautiful rain
Ignoring all the pain
Steadfast and strong
Belting out in true love song
Dancing smiles
Angel's flight free
Grateful for loves lessons
Hurt, passion, and all its blessings
It teaches you,
And it teaches me
Loves teacher
Has set my heart free

Forgiving

I'm sorry for any pain
I may have caused you
I have grown to forgive you
And hope you forgive me to
I didn't mean everything that I said
Things appear to be working
Themselves out
Thus, you can rest your weary head
Not exactly sure what else I should say
I only feel
I'm truly over all of it
And tomorrow is a new day
In honor of Michelle

Until I'm Whole

So many nice men come and go
Where they go
I just don't know
I briefly let them in my world
Then kick them out
My hearts healing an old love
That reciprocates only in doubt
Often love is offered
I can't give in
If I follow and trust my heart
Then I have to win
Loves always a battle when one
Party gives up
Toughing it out, in hopes of luck
Something good is coming of this
When it is my heart that will be missed
To precious to be denied
So sad over a lie
Though I'm glad my heart still loves
Cherishing
What the good Lord gave me from above
Never doubting my bountiful soul
Counting down the days
Until I'm whole

Funny

Funny how things turn
Out this way
Funny how you learned
Love was already there
Every step of the way
Funny how you turned me down
Now, things are spun around
Funny how much time
Has been wasted
My love
You once tasted
Funny how it may be to late
Funny you expected me to wait
Now I know where your priorities were
Weed and those stupid girls
Your friends gave me reason
To see you as a PUNK!
Funny you actually believed
Good was gonna come out of
Where most of Cowlitz county men
Had already placed there junk

In The End

A man can befriend

But when he is gone

GOD is still there in the end

Through it all thick and thin

He is the one always within

GOD is who you are

Every dream you ever have

Wished upon a star

Answers your prayers

Without hint of fear

Holds your hand, hugs you, and wipes your tears

He'll put the pressure on,

So careful what you ask for

Yet, trust his support Heaven and beyond

If you've been in love with a man

He does something for you

Though nothing close to what GOD can,

For if he does it may be odd

Keep him close

Because he must be a man of GOD

Missing without doubts

When a companion has come and gone

One trust remains all along

And your love may be a very good friend though

GOD is the one there, in the end though

Friendship Is the End

You cannot capture my heart today
Stand in line is all I have to say
You think you are the one for me
I may be single but my heart is not yet free
Nor' will it ever be
To choose whom I want or wish
I'm in love with my own future
Please believe this
Nothing personal to you at all
Because I do like it
I'm not even thinking about you
Yet, you care enough to call
No man can give me what I can
No man ever needs to guide me by the hand
I don't mean to hurt you, but friends is all we can do
You ask something of me that I cannot provide
Respect the facts though, I never lied?
Told you from the gate
For me love may be to late
It has abandoned me long ago
I still have dreams and goals
For my kids and I though
For now I'd like to keep you
My new found friend
Trust that love is not our future
Friendship is the end

Over You Today

Not in love with me

So give me closure

Set my heart free

It's only within yourself

That you're unhappy

I knew I shouldn't have

Trusted you

Doesn't matter

Because I'm the one who

Did all the working out too

Me and you against the world

Huh, yeah

I guess I was a foolish girl

I'm not afraid to express myself

And how I feel

While you run from

Any emotion to real

This emotional conflict

I couldn't ever depict

The emotions you avoid and escape

All the while my heart

You forcefully scrape

I don't want you anyway

Nothing is serious

In the game you play

So what I acted out the way I did

Anyone would

Stumped by an arrogant pig

I wasn't just holding on

You lead me there

For that, you're more than wrong

And yes it is true

I believed a lot of you

Not my problem you're addicted

To gambling and pills

Chase easy woman for cheap thrills

You have never tired

Everything to make it work

You kept lying

Causing more hurt

If I was emotionally unstable

It's because you were emotionally disrespectful & unable

Of course I was angry disappointed and confused

After all it was my heart you used and abused

Ignore mine, not care, and fight

That's what you choose

Your fear of commitment is no big secret

I don't want you anymore

So please just keep it

So what? I thought you would come around

But, like mama always said

You can't keep a guy

That only wants to play around

I don't need to apologize

You have lost me

Look into my eyes

You're more cold than anyone would ever think

This is it

You have pushed me to the brink

Accepting all the lies

Shoved off the edge, I now fly

Your only explanation is the way I act

Pshht! Damn! What do you do? Under attack?

For Valentines Day you gave me

More bruised

I'm not sure why I put up with your abuse

Now that I know the truth, I'm done

I'm stronger than you-So have what you want

You who fears me

You wouldn't even give closure

Where is your sanity?

I do get sad and yes I will mourn

Though I'm picking up the pieces

That you have torn

You send mixed signals

With your jealousy and rage

Please just release me

From your cold hearted, steal, cage

Never again will I want to

Hold, touch or kiss you again

You are so unworthy

And only some where

I have already been

This is not an easy

Thing for me to say

But I'm truly over you today

Wasted Time

Now that I know the whole truth

I will be more than fine

Somewhere between content and divine

Just don't fall back to me

Without something extraordinary

I will not exploit myself

"Be quiet and sit my love on a shelf"

My heart is meant to be

Shared and seen

I must admit, your method was keen

I'm happy, I'm strong

And so great full

GOD showed me you were wrong

You lied to me along with others

And don't repent

It's alright, I don't need you

I'm perfectly competent

I'm not a man hater

Or complete feminist

Just, dealing with men who act childish

Is not at the top of my list

I'm healing through a lot of rhyme

Thus, you weren't a complete waste of time

Frienifit

I know you want a piece of me

Though I'm no ones sex

To be a memory

My love is never in vain

I'm being honest

Because I refuse to cause intentional pain

I distance myself, as a reminder

To keep love on a shelf

You're so sweet

There is no one else I have been so proud to meet

The honest friendship we share

I adore sharing with you

Knowing you deeply care

I admire how open and thoughtful

You are

No need to interrupt that with sex

I'm confident either way

We will last far

I'd rather keep you forever

Just within my heart

Maintaining open, loyal honesty

And never part

No matter how many

Miles between us there are

So young, so fresh

Frienifit, you're the <u>best!</u>

Handicap

I would always love you

Even if you were handicap

Now that I realize you are

It makes me laugh

Emotionally crippled that's what you are

I know I held up my end of the bargain

While your out

Scanning the bar

I have faults

Yes I do

Where the fuck are you

Living your lies

The sacrifice is parts of

My loyal and true heart dies

You promised the same

Yet, in our grey cloud

You're the cause of the rain

The pain

I now know that what you are

Sincerely emotionally insane

Your love for me….lust

All of it in vain

Don't know how to

Emotionally invest

That's the truth

Fuck the rest

Family

I guess the future is the past
Family has been there from the
First day till the last
Nothing else matter's in between
Wasted time or the
Bitter memories
It has all been heard and seen
No other love matters
Before or after that
Linked together forever
Like it or not
They are there for you
When your mind appears to be gone
The one's who really love you
Reveal themselves before too long
Family is the whole in the middle
Forming everything on the edge
Supportive of all things
Positive within your head
Blood, bonds, or just ties
Are the foundation
Holding this unique shape
To everyone inside
Family is the symbol of love
Our heart
It shouldn't be denied

I guess my future is my past

Family has been there
From the first day till the last
Nothing else matters
In between
Wasted time and bitter memories
It's all been heard and seen
Before and after that
Linked together forever
Like it or not
It's whose there for you
When your mind is gone
The ones who really love you
Revealed all along

Danger

Ashamed in danger
All the pain
Inflicted, twisted to anger
Love came early
And now it's best 2 leave
Only give back
What you receive
See love usually
Arrives late
Someone has misunderstood
What they thought was fate
Choosing not to change
The levels on the scales
The events they will go
And allowance of range
If they wanted to lead
Someone else would've followed
If you only hold one in your heart
It is hallow
Ashamed of a reaction
Because of the attraction
It might be wrong
If even by a small fraction
Deserve only what you give
Practice how you want to live
Easy to give up cuz
Causing hurt to someone else
Sometimes hurts more
Invested future in store
Equal the scale by dropping anger
No longer in danger
Heart so protected
Strongest, bad ass chick
Self-elected

No Longer

No longer going to pretend

Now that it's the end

I will now begin

To give my love

Let that someone special in

Have him take me by the hand

Tell him my deepest trust

He'll understand

No worries anymore

Worlds of possibilities opened

Because we have closed that door

No longer consume my

Worries or thoughts

No longer in my head

No longer my enemy

Just in my heart as dead

So now go away

No longer a part of me

Just an old friend

I once wished would stay

No longer mine

Though for your happiness I will pray

So long as you do the same

No longer are you a special name

Because we are no longer, I have found happiness

And fame

Hole in My Heart

Somewhere near the middle
Of my heart
Lies the spot
Wounded and feeling forgot
Leading so deep within my soul
Dark, empty and unknown
Though love peeks through
Every time I meet
A love I never knew
Cannot touch, smell or taste
Everything that was true
Turned on me
With lies, deceit and hate
I let that place in my heart win
For a future with
Barricaded walls caving in
Is it love or sin?
Let it go or
Define where "we" begins
In the middle of my heart
There lies a spot
Though it's forgiven
My heart has not forgot

Loyalty

What does it consist of?

Does one give themselves up?

If they are in love

The world turns

In temptation

Causes so many stomachs to churn

Thrown arms

Open so wide

Same as pushing your heart open

No secrets to hide

Forgiven is everything

Loyalty = what's giving back?

What they bring

Is nothing more than what you need

It could be all you wanted but couldn't have

Though you begged and pleaded

When one takes

That precious part of themselves back

Loyalty in pride is always left

But, what is that?

Spider Bite

Once bit and twice shy

Is there any particular reason why?

If it's not about relationship and love

Then waste not time

End now with a wink and a hug

No need for you to return

Don't worry about me

I live and I learn

I don't need sympathy

Or any explanations

Save the semantics for

Your next has been

You're the one that said you

Were looking for something more

Excuse me…. I must go

Excuses to me, have always been such a bore

You may have freaked your self out

Due to immaturity

No worries once bit and twice shy

Come a dime a dozen to me

I know there is more than your kind out there for me to see

Hence, I'm letting you go

Because I know that it's right

Sorry, you were scared of by a spider bite.

In honor of Mr. Fissell

Yes, I just called you a pussy ass.

Hearts Sorrow

In my hearts of sorrow
If I'm never loved again
Will they know I gave my best?
By tomorrow
Will they believe that?
It was enough
Will they know?
It was about love
In my hearts of sorrow
If I never get to give true love again
Will someone close by be willing?
To lend and barrow
Will they let me believe it is true?
Will they wait for me to
Let them down easy too
In my hearts of sorrow
With GOD
I'm loved yesterday, today, and, tomorrow
Always loving
Even in my hearts of sorrow

You Wish

No need for closure
I find it poetry form of exposure
Isn't it true?
You wished us to stay with you
Weren't you sad?
Because we moved away
You wished you didn't treat us so bad
Aren't you angry?
You wished you could hold me every night
We all knew it was true
You wish you could've treated me right
You wish all your problems would go away
You wish your anger would stay at bay
You wish your life to change
Yet, you wish it all stays the same
You wish me to see your love deep down inside
You wish you didn't run and hide
You wish I didn't leave
You wish all your stories I believed
You wish I didn't know you so well
You wish our relationships didn't get pushed to hell
You wish you weren't under a poison tree
You wish weren't so angry
You wish anger and fear weren't a part of all this
You wish we were still
In love with just one kiss

Jekyll

Write a poem about you?
Is that what you really want?
My homie? Fuck you punk!
You know what you did, what you lied about
And to whom
I speculate you're another uncertain man
Who made a bad decision?
Because you assumed
You thought something of me that
Simply wasn't true
Believing rumors
Or that was just a cop-out
So you could do those deceitful things you do
That's what I believe it must have been
Because those thoughts of me are severely misdirected
I really don't have the time to waste
Struggling to hold our friendship together
Is the same as building a home with paste?
I shouldn't have to work so hard
For you to recognize I am a great friend
If you are giving back what I give
Contentment through it all
Is the light at the end?
Now that I have said what I have to say
Seriously, be a true friend
Or get the hell out of my way

Hyde

Sank in to Eden with you
Touched smelled and tasted
My forbidden fruit
Cried alone in a church
God by my side
I will bread words to you here
Save your eyes you will need them
It is finally time for you to see
I am not here for you
Projecting on you, you are now free
Been swept away
The greatest of teacher's
Do not hesitate
Left here alone
Chained by fate
I alone befriend you
I alone care about you
I alone love you
Set to sail off with bliss
Though now fearful
Unworthy of a woman like me
is not the end of this?

Fallen Core

I promise to never forget

The day we kissed or even met

Or the day we fell so deep

And vowed true love to keep

The sky may fall

And the stars may even too

But I have and always do

Love you

Though its not up to me anymore

If you want me in your life

I long to be a wife

You can find a way to put

And keep me there

It's your heart you must spare

You need to trust if I say I love you

Because I will always mean it

Even though a love like ours

It seems too good to be true

To good to leave, and to bad to stay

So be it, what can I say?

Hard to swallow when Im

The yin to your yang

I'll get over it

It's no thang!

Fallen from the core

It's to hard to hold on anymore

The Reasons You Didn't Last

Made your self look grand
Knelt down in front of the church
Asked for my hand
I denied you because you didn't understand
Tore my poetry away
Asked me why I waste my time
On it every single day
Threw my collection in the trash
Stole my jewelry and money
To sit at the poker table
Not to mention come home with no cash
Told your friends I was the babysitter
You cheated on the Sally talk show
Just to avoid taking responsibility
Looking like a chimo
The thought of you telling my child there was no Santa
Was contemptuous

My daughter got more attention than yours

You and she were always jealous

Telling her she wasn't as pretty as

I told her she was

Saying ludicrous things

Just because

Take my clothes even my panties

Crying about how you need me

Oh please, have some wine with that cheese

Throw a burrito in my face

Because of your insecurities

You were quickly replaced

Tried to get away with my brand new car

Took you to court

Obviously you didn't make it that far

Using cocaine behind my back

While I took care of your children

These are the reasons

My love for you lacked

Emotionally Sued

I know you here what I have to say
Unfortunately, to me it's not a game
You are not listening although you can hear
Yippidy, yippidy, blah, blah, yackity, yack, in your ear
That's all it is to you
Consider yourself emotionally sued
If it were possible than I would
Because you no longer provide to me what you should
You claim to love me though you are scared inside
You don't know how or why
Then when confronted you simply tell lies
Though, in reality it's only to yourself
I want you I stand by you
But you need some help
If you're serious about me
Learn to love yourself and us right
If not
Move out of tunnel vision
I am gearing towards the light

A Strong Woman

A strong woman
Is one who feels deeply
And loves fiercely
Her tears flow
Just as abundantly
As her laughter
She puts time in plus some after
A strong woman is both
Soft and powerful
She is both practical and spiritual
When under pressure knows how to keep her cool
A strong woman
In her own essence
Is greatly valued to all the world
A strong woman is
What every woman should be
A strong woman I know
Is me

I Officially Miss You

I don't know you at all

But, when I find you

I'm prepared to fall

For everything you do for me

Is reciprocated

Where your pain can be released

All the things you told me

The days that you hold me

When I'm consumed inside of you

Your love encased in me so true

Where age is just a number too

Nothing compared to

What our love can do

My thoughts become emotionally spun

Because together, we are the only one

Our hearts beat faster in depth

Sweetest taste of fiery kisses kept

No such thing as lying

No such thing as sadness and crying

Every single fight

Means something because

We know how everything is alright

When I meet you I know it will be true

For, there is no one that does it like you do

I'm not talking about thug love

I'm talking about the whole in my heart

That you and cupid shot and dug

That leads me to this love and bliss

Hot, yet tender kiss

That tells me it is you

I officially miss

Good Friend

Never took over my responsibility
Only suggested it was okay to be me
Always helped me out whenever I asked
Comforting me when I would dwell on the past
Rarely, hinting desires
Of anything in return
Those other typical guys would
Friends is really all we are
You simply understood
Grateful for you in my life
Praying for you to find that special girl
That wants to be your wife
Always up to share companionship
With a drink meal or snack
Telling me how great I'm
Reminding me to never look back
A good friend I would never replace
Through down and out
Or drinking for days
You brought back laughter, joy
And the smiles I wear on my face
Take pride in generosity you give
Teaching me who's most important
God, me and of course my kids
Showed me how to be grateful for what I have
Proved to me I could keep going
Even though I was sullen and sad
I truly trust you
That's one thing that makes
You my good friend
Our bond shall never end

Self-Esteem Boat

Everything I have said about you
They have retaliated back to me
I have now been through it all
That hook and line
Can and does cause us to sink
When Karma puts us at the bottom
With no where else to be
I begin to question my faith and sanity
Surround myself with love
Honor myself with a hug
We made it through another day
Telling evil to go away
Staying a float
While other's attempt to vandalize us
In our self-esteem boat

I realize we have more in common than originally thought
Sometimes men in life will force us crazy
It's not always just what we are taught
I see you are doing better hope you stay strong
You and I, We're both in the wrong
It's all over and now everything is ok
You deserve to have your babies
For that I will continue to pray.
In Honor of Michelle

Virtual Reality

The things that once made me whole
Have currently left my soul
Battles and wars is the only place I have control
I hide away
Because the courts say
My daughter so significant
Can't exist anymore
Suffering, agony, triumph galore
Demonic behaviors constantly
Knocking at my door
Privacy and piece of mind
Impossible to seek and find
Left with my own entertainment
Wasting time well spent
Blood daughter missing, left in pain
Everything I believed in
Appears to be nothing more
Than lies and everything insane
Yet, guns and destruction
That is where I have control
Without her, no one
Including myself wants "that" me anymore
Destroyed is everything
In actuality
The only thing left is my virtual reality
- In Honor of Jason and Taylor

Jaded

You can think it's cute that I
Call myself jaded
Keep all the dark clouds to yourself
Grey's all shaded
Too bad you never learned
What that word means
Because you were to busy in school
Getting faded
Gracing everyone with your so called charm
Telling people
Trust me, I mean no harm
Here is the truth to everyone
Red flag, sound the alarm
I am on my way back to
Where I am supposed to be
And I'm doing it all on my own two feet
Go ahead, claim it
You left me?
You're gone because you treated
Me and mine disrespectfully
Half way is where
The Lord and my true friends meet thee
I am laughing now
Jaded,
I take my bow

Sabotage

Letting go
Of everything that is good
When it happens you don't
See things like you should
I am sorry you choose to live that way
I say a special prayer
For you every time I pray
Then I see you
Making the same mistakes
Over and over again
Though, I won't give up hope
Because that's in me
The Christian
Not for us just for you
Like a mirage
You should be illegal
Because everything you touch
You seem to sabotage

Me, Myself, and I

I am going to love me
The best I can
I salute the ones who
Couldn't handle it and ran
The alarm fires off
Within my heart
Strength inside
No one can tear me apart
Mind brilliant and free
No longer bogged down
By men in history
Body comfortable and secure
I am me
Don't really need Gucci, Channel, or Couture
Spirit real sincere and light
Try to break me apart
With any kind of fight
You can't
Me, myself and I
We are tight

GOD

Which way do I tide

High or low

I will abide

So long as you say it's right

My savior

It's no longer necessary to fight

I truly give in

I'm not going to plead

You know how I have been

Grasping all my pain

Flowing abundantly through my veins

When I don't resist your power

I find comfort in you

Every waking hour

We have exhausted

The agony, delusion and tears

I'm so glad GOD you are all I fear

The Bad Potion

If I had to do it all over
I would still choose you
To be my daddy once more
Even if I lost you again
It would be worth all the tears
In the world and all the hearts torn
You were my sunshine
Now my skies are gray
I loved and bonded to you
Because you knew
How to play my tears away
I was proud to be
Your little girl
Sometimes we did argue
But you were always my whole world
You treated me as your own
Even if our time was cut short
Like my real daddy, you left me alone
My heart was completely crushed
But momma says
Nothing loved is ever lost
And you were loved so much
I cherish trips to the ocean
The ones you obviously forgot
When you drank the bad potion
I want to see you Jason
It's been seven years
That bad potion
Kept you from my loving heart so dear
I think the bad potion was inside of your beer.

Took A Long Time

Took along a time

To get to this spot

I remember maximizing

How "Godly" you were in my heart

To merely nothing more than a dot

Ask me? Am I loving you today?

Or forever, I am not

It took a really long time

To get to this spot

How I loved you so

Damn, I must have forgot

Though, I easily remember all the tears

That I had to blot

It took a really, really, long time to get to this spot

I remember how you manipulated

Mine and my daughter's mind

When she was just a tot

How I treated you like a king

When you are by far, NOT

It took a really really really long time to get to this spot

Not caring was something I wasn't capable of

Yet, was determined to top

Leaving you in my past

Never going to stop

Damn, it took a really, really, really long time to get to this spot

Treasured Memories

The ones I have loved and still do
Cherished memories
And the pain we can't undo
No longer captive of what I cannot have
I treasure you all and our past
Every documented memo
Within my heart
Valued highly in the
Back of my mind
Even the reasons to the questions
We couldn't ever find
I adore you for letting me into your world
I appreciate you for loving my girls
Even have respect for the arguments
That we have had
You helped me grow
I have no choice except to be glad
You are people I loved deeply
Who becomes a memory
The memory becomes a treasure
I'll always hold apart of you inside of me
You – my past
Will always be my favorite
Treasured Memories

Nothing Left To Say

What do we put ourselves through this for?
When we simply didn't
Love each other anymore
All I could do for you
You tried to do for me too
There is nothing either of us
Can say or do
To keep each other loving true
We had our pride and
Caused a lot of pain
Unfortunately though,
There really, is nothing left to say?

Words

You can say them soft
Or write them off
You can twist the meaning
Or leave you audience phening
You can toss them up
Or slam them down
Create a smile or cause a frown
Use them to your advantage
Or set some ones heart free
You can expand them
Or let them be
Words are more powerful
Than most even know
Change the meaning when
Expressing them
Quiet, loud, fast and slow
Meaning of words change
Happy to derange
Meaning of words in rhyme
Discovering the meanings
Also change over time
Organized, scattered, or slurred
I have a thang for words

Buddies

The suede shod on your feet
Laughing eyes
The dark brown to your hair
Infectious grin
I see you standing there
You are placed in my heart, and in my mind
Like the glided cages with you
Me standing beside
Talk of places we had been
Never where we will go
The cycles, I don't get to ride
Emotion I have to wish to abide
Reading briefs on your beer
I am deep for you still
Year after year
Walking in the rain
Blowing through the storm
With snoop dog riders in the new truck
Still commitment refrained

Every time you would talk with her
I'd want to jog and hide
Unable to change the subject
I trembled to pieces inside
Longing for you to look at me
When we would share an embrace
Who am I to say such things?
You only want me for a friend
So, I'll sit back and play it light
If I must just be a pal
I guess that's what I will be
Although, just being near you
Does curious things to me
But, I will be your friend,
I can pretend
That is all you are to me
Maybe someday,
I will discover why
Buddies, is all we were meant to be

Loved By Me

You show that you don't
Want to lose me
Is it true, could it be?
If so than hold on tight
For I am so many times
Close to slipping away
Forever in the night
Curious, even when your eyes
Are wide open during the day light
No longer can your ignorance be accounted for
Tap into your emotion
Open up, explore
Opportunities await you there
Tired of seeing your soul
Captive, it's just not fair
Erase the toxins from your mind
Wrath about leaving too
Demons inside
You're well alive
So far, not dead
Live up to your awesome potential
Remember, keep it simple
Like your dad said
You want to be "us" in unity
Then love yourself

More than you want to be loved by me

Inglorious Morning

He looked into her eyes
Saw his future
Came closer, thoughts of disguise
Uncertain, yet driven
Connection the Lord handed
And given
Just received
She attentively stared
Back into his
And walked away
So, what does it mean?
Perhaps, she has witnessed her future
That was her past
Scared off by a back flash
Sworn to herself
Never to be jaded again
Reminded,
Morning glorious
Never happened

The Change Begins With Me Disclaimer

All relationships have problems, right? It's the good times that matter most, right? Or have you like I, been locked in an unworthy disrespectful relationships?

I am totally drained from the yo-yo affect and the emotional roller coaster rides. I would feel so happy and full of energy when they would be attentive, caring and loving. When I loved them I loved them strong, so it wasn't hard for them to make me feel lighthearted, or full of joy, when they would behave in this manner. Especially considering that I was the one usually giving the attention. Though in just an instant they could make my heart sink straight to the ground beneath me. The disappointments I have experienced over and over because they could make me feel so important one day, only to turn around the next day saying unkind or the opposite of what they had just said the day before, avoiding me and my emotions. When I would see them again, they could give me "the look" or that certain stare I call mean mugging. This only meant they new they were about to be called out on there crap. It was better I didn't say anything, or bring up "drama" right? Typically at this point would become an obvious long string of withdraw.

Strong woman that I am I convince myself over and over that I was strong enough to handle the droughts of them. I was addicted to the "mystery like" outcomes, although, they were ultimately oh' so predicable. They were and are unworthy, unpredictable, unappreciative men. I wasn't going to give up easily. I would figure "if I just stick things out". And never give up (we) could have a perfect relationship. I have stuck through these relationships this far, and they have too, so… they must be worthy of all I have, right? Well, in the last relationship, I did just that I gave ALL I could give, until one day I just realized I didn't have anything left to give him he had taken so much. It felt like just bitter memories left because he took and took and took. It was a rare occasion for him to give back. I realized the negative emotions of these kinds of men far out weighed the positive ones. I became very insecure, weak, lost, jealous and at times obsessive of what I had invested into the relationship. I was beyond angry.

Something had to change; I desperately started seeking solutions to my issues, that I undoubtedly already had the answers too. I wanted to show them what a huge mistake they made in letting me go, I wanted them to want me for the rest of their lives, even though I didn't want them anymore. Also, I thought I couldn't give up until they had shown me consistency with respect or love that I knew I deserved. Although I knew chances of this happening were very slim. I thought if I could just remind them how much I did and that I was the best thing that happened to them, they would "see the light".

Reminiscing now, how I couldn't eat, sleep, or even think straight for that matter, crying and feeling abandoned. I would check my text, e-mails, or missed calls periodically. All of it seems very pathetic in retrospect. But, I did frequently look at photo's, and imagine in my head the sex we had or could have in the future, anything that was emotionally connected or shared. Even the arguments, the "I do love you" as constant reminder or reassurance that I was the only one or at least the biggest potential option in their life at the time. Looking back it was very arrogant of me to think I could change the prideful street hustler, the emotionally retarded guy, the best friend, the married man, the guy with girlfriend issues, the one with a commitment phobia. Who was I? What the heck was I thinking?

All the signs while beginning these relationships were there I just chose to ignore them all while being the "understanding girlfriend. That one that flees away with his friends, the other who would say things "are getting better" in his marriage or relationship, or things were "worse", how bout the one who stops saying and showing affection after he "thinks or knows" that he has your heart. The one who would say call me at such and such time, and doesn't answer or make any effort to call you back. All those things that are present at the beginning of any relationship aren't always fizzled out because of something you did or didn't do. See the pattern; it's most likely his own issues. See, I thought, I must have been the cause because in the arguments that is what they would say. So, naturally I would take the blame and justify their actions or behavior for them. I was very good at this.

I loved them to much not too, or did I? I wanted to be blind that these relationships had potential to end. After all, they didn't mean to be disrespectful? I wasn't very good with change like that in any relationship. I later learned that we all grow in different ways day by day, there are no guarantees in life or love for that matter there is not a map to life or an answer sheet to all of loves unanswered questions. Some couples grow apart as they grow older other's grow together with any change in situations. Growing means change, changing is the only promise life or maybe even love offer's us. The more I grew emotionally and mentally through these "loves" the more acquainted with pain I became. The reason is because obviously the unworthy and toxic relationships themselves were hurtful and healing from them was too. I had to look, face, and fix the truths about myself. #1 I can not change them, fix there problems, or prescribe a remedy to there issues.

Nothing is ever going to be just right; there is always challenges, obstacles, and not so perfect conditions. While life continues to automatically change. I had an option to grow because growth is optional it is also an opportunity if you choose to give up on the person who has not treated you the way they should. I make choices on a daily basis and still often struggle with which one is the wise one. Although, I am confident the intent is to always move forward, even if you have to take a step back to look inside from the outside. I would tend to see more clearly this way even with stigmatism. I would think about the big picture while observing. This is where the beginning of the end hurt the most too. I had to accept that these relationships were not and are not meant to be. These men were not going to change just because they "loved" me. This is something I had to let go.

No matter how much I thought I "loved" them, or believed they "actually" loved or respected me too, it just wasn't so. Bitter sweet, I know. I had to be true to myself, something new since I previously was so busy being true to them. No matter how bad I wanted to be loved or needed by them. I honestly couldn't put my heart into them anymore. So, I took myself out. It was after and only after I totally let go, that my higher power showed me exactly the what's why's and who's I was holding onto guiding me to grounded evidence allowing me to make decisions on weather or not they were really worth holding onto. Wow, talk about a confidence boost. The confidence didn't come from all the answer's though. Ironically, it came from being completely open to all the questions and possible outcomes. Never truly knowing after this point what they thought or felt about me as a person, because you know what? Suddenly it didn't matter anymore.

Loneliness became a factor for me that I feared for a long time certainly. I unwillingly learned to embrace it with a clear mind. This stage in my life there was immense growth. I could achieve more due to being able to self-assert or evaluate my (true-self). No interruptions. I stopped regretting my past, it's mistakes and became hungry for my future. Instead of allowing myself to "die trying" to figure out the ex's / there issues or why they couldn't love me anymore. I could focus on getting me back.

I began to be thankful that I was able to show a love to each person I had been evolved with. Each one of them in a way that they hadn't really experienced before or had simply forgotten existed. I got to share my children with men who wanted to be father's and weren't or couldn't be. I got to build families for them that they may now only hope and pray to see again someday. I got to share my heart even in small pieces with yet, another human being. I am so grateful to be brave enough to eventually do it again when the Lord says he is the right one. Not just anyone.

For now, I am responsible for my own happiness when I put as much time and energy into (me) as I did other's. Man, Oh' Man, I really feel loved. I am a good lover and need no validations. If I ever thought I wanted an old love back. I think I may have found it. When I look in the mirror everyday I tell myself I am worthy of me. I love me, I am going to ignore other's issues and problems, I am not going to burden my heart with what they are unable to give me. If I allow myself to get sucked in by any of them, I am settling. I will not settle for less than what I am worth or what I am willing to give. I am not miserable and do not need it's company, I will continue to improve myself for my God, me and my children first. Though the change begins with me, drastic changes are never easy or overnight.

My past truly has made me who I am and will be in the future. I really am grateful; I will continue to be the best I can be and do the best I can do. I do not want to make the same mistakes and if I do I will learn from them, I want to keep looking ahead at these brighter days. I will accept loneliness now as a blueprint to my success ahead and build my future based on my past. Again, I thank everyone who has assisted in my growth to make me who I am today. I was fine before and knew it. Today I will never get over myself because; I am amazing and know it. I will continue reaching my highest potential with or without help and support. To the woman who relates to what I have written about; whether it is a romantic relationship that has failed you, or a parent who abandoned you. "The change begins with you", you are beautiful, powerful, and have the potential to be and teach and have strength. Best wishes, with angel blessings.

About The Book

It's about the sloppiness of real life, relationships, love, and heartache. How crazy a single person can alter your mind to act when it was supposed to be forever and how forever sometimes never lasts, a glimpse of what it feels like to know your alive but can't feel your pulse? Searching and seeking for it because you refuse to be the one with the broken spirit. It's about no matter how much you have been hurt, not giving up, getting through the bitter and finding what works for you, in your life. Being true, telling the truth, and moving on. Wanting and needing to have a voice connected to the emotions that the emotionally insulting person/people chose to ignore. It's about friends who stand by your side and remind you how beautiful you are and how worthy you are and should be if you can find it within yourself to stop believing in the person that hurts you the most.

Printed in the United States
by Baker & Taylor Publisher Services